TABLE OF CONTENTS

IN CHURCH FOR 40 YEARS AND NOT KNOWING GOD

Escaping Tradition to Truly Know God

PHILIP GUENAGA

BIBLE SCRIPTURES

Unless otherwise noted, Scripture quotations are taken from the
New King James Version®. Copyright © 1982 by Thomas Nelson.
Used by permission. All rights reserved.

Published in the United States of America by

Spirit Media, Inc.
https://spiritmedia.us

Spirit Media and our logos are trademarks of
Spirit Media, Inc.
8045 Arco Corporate Drive STE 130
Raleigh, NC 27617
1-888-800-3744

Religion | Christian Books & Bibles | Spiritual Growth

Paperback ISBN: 979-8-89307-204-4
eBook ISBN: 979-8-89307-205-1
PDF ISBN: 979-8-89307-206-8
Library of Congress Control Number: 20259277605

Acknowledgement

I met Philip Guenaga a few years ago at a gym that we frequented. We had a lot in common when we talked about the things of God. We quickly became like brother and sister, as you know, they don't always agree.

But this was different, our conversations were thought-provoking and interesting. We each shared our perspective on various topics and sometimes we would even pick up where we left off the next day.

It was clear to me from that point the passion for the Word of God that Philip had in our discussions. We started throwing around the idea of him writing a book. He gave me such a hard time every time we talked about it. He gave me several excuses about why he could not write, why he was not sure he should write, on and on and on.

I am proud to be able to say today that I am excited that he completed the book that you are about to read, and excited that you will receive insight that you may have not experienced before.

DR. PRECIOUS TAYLOR

FOREWORD

I want to add a word about this book and the author. I have known Philip Guenaga for 34 years. This book is, first, an act of love, and second, a true understanding of God's word. Philip loves the Lord beyond human understanding. This book is dedicated to those that are searching for a genuine relationship with the giver of life, Jesus Christ.

As a young man Philip had an experience with God that carried him through difficult times. He never forgot that experience, no matter where he was. When Philip came to Rolla, Missouri in 1986 and attended the church I pastored, I immediately saw his consecration. For the next two and a half years, he was a great blessing to our church.

I believe I can say with confidence, this book will be a blessing to you.

Open your heart as you read this book and let God speak to you.

PASTOR LARRY THORNHILL

PERSONAL THANKS

I want to give a special thanks to my Pastor Larry Thornhill who pastored me when I was stationed in Ft. Leonard Wood, Missouri. He is the one who encouraged me to write. I also want to give thanks to my special friend Dr. Precious Taylor who also has pushed me to write and has also gone the extra mile to edit my book.

And of course, my lovely wife Reyna Guenaga.

Thank you all and I love you all,
Your humble servant,

PHILIP GUENAGA

Introduction

AN INVITATION TO DEEPER STUDY

There's a profound difference between knowing about God and truly knowing Him. Most of us, especially those raised in religious traditions, have accumulated knowledge about God— but genuine relationship with Him often remains elusive.

My own journey began in a deeply religious household. Through various denominational experiences, I discovered something curious: while Bible stories remained consistent across different churches, interpretations of salvation varied dramatically. Some emphasized baptism while others dismissed it; some required speaking in tongues while others considered it unnecessary.

This book invites you on a journey of personal discovery. Rather than accepting traditional interpretations without question, I encourage you to examine Scripture with fresh eyes. You might be surprised by what you find when you look closely at familiar passages.

— Chapter 1 —

WHAT WERE THEIR REAL NAMES?

The True Name of Adam and Eve

Let's begin with something that might surprise you. In most religious traditions I've encountered, people naturally assume that the first man and woman were named Adam and Eve. This seems so universally accepted that few would think to question it.

However, when we examine the biblical text closely, we find an interesting detail that's often overlooked.

> Genesis 5:2 states: "Male and female created he them; and blessed them, and called their name Adam, on the day when they were created."

According to this passage, God named them both Adam. The name "Eve" was actually given by the man, not by God. We can trace this in the text: Adam first called her "Woman" (Genesis 2:23), and only later gave her the name "Eve" (Genesis 3:20).

While it's true that the Bible frequently refers to them as "Adam and Eve" throughout Scripture, this appears to reflect the human perspective that developed over time rather than God's original intention. From God's perspective, as stated in Genesis 5:2, they would have both been called "Adam." The change in naming seems to have come from human initiative rather than divine command.

Reflection Questions

- How might our understanding of gender roles change if we considered that God originally gave both man and woman the same name?
- What other familiar Bible "facts" might benefit from closer examination of the original text?

Notes

_____

_____

_____

_____

_____

_____

_____

_____

_____

_____

_____

_____

Chapter 2

THE COMPLETE IMAGE

The Real Image of God

This discovery leads to another intriguing question: if God created man (Adam) in His image, who was He referring to—the man, or the woman?

Both were called Adam, and before the fall they were equal in God's eyes. Genesis 1:27 says: "So God created man in his own image, in the image of God created them; male and female created him."

The end of that scripture is significant—they were both created in His image. Yet God does not have a physical body as we do. So what might "His image" mean?

Through prayer and reflection, I believe I received insight from God into this question. Consider the attributes we often associate with different genders: women frequently embody love, patience, nurturing, and compassion, while men often express justice, order, protection, and discipline.

What if God embodies all of these qualities perfectly? Perhaps it's in the union of marriage that humanity most fully reflects God's complete image—two complementary aspects of His nature united to form a fuller reflection of who He is.

This perspective illuminates other passages, such as Genesis 2:24: "Therefore shall a man leave his father and his mother, and shall cleave unto his wife: and they shall be one flesh."

Rather than understanding this literally, could this "one flesh" refer to the completion of God's image? This would help explain the spiritual significance of marriage and why Scripture places such importance on this union.

Consider This:

The image of God might be one of the most powerful forces on earth. When demons encountered Jesus, they recognized Him immediately—even before He spoke (Matthew 8:28-34). There's an authority in God's image that spiritual forces recognize and respect.

If married couples truly represent God's complete image, this might explain why marriages face such spiritual opposition. When a husband and wife stand in unity and agreement, they reflect something powerful about God's nature. As Matthew 18:19 promises: "If two of you shall agree on earth as touching any thing that they shall ask, it shall be done for them of my Father which is in heaven."

For Further Study:

- How does this perspective change your understanding of marriage?
- What other biblical concepts might become clearer when viewed through this lens?

Notes

_____

_____

_____

_____

_____

_____

_____

_____

_____

_____

_____

_____

—— *Chapter 3* ——

REEXAMINING
FAMILIAR BLAME

A Different Perspective on the Fall

Throughout history, many have placed primary blame for humanity's fall on Eve. But when we examine the biblical account carefully, a different picture emerges—one that challenges this traditional interpretation.

Let's trace the sequence of events:

The Original Command:

In Genesis 2:15-17, God placed Adam in the garden with specific instructions not to eat from the tree of the knowledge of good and evil. Notably, Eve hadn't been created yet (Genesis 2:18-23).

A Crucial Detail:

God told Adam only that he couldn't *eat* from the tree—nothing about not *touching* it. Yet when Eve encounters the serpent, she says God commanded them not to touch the tree (Genesis 3:3).

The Question:

Where did this additional restriction come from? Since Eve wasn't present for the original conversation, Adam must have relayed God's instructions to her. But somewhere in that communication, touching the tree became forbidden too.

A New Perspective:

When Eve touched the fruit, nothing happened. When she ate it, there was still nothing. The consequences only began when Adam ate—at which point "their eyes were opened."

This suggests the command was specifically for Adam, the one who had received it directly. Eve's actions had no immediate consequence because the prohibition wasn't originally directed at her.

Implications for Understanding:

• Could this perspective change how we view responsibility in relationships?

• How might this affect our understanding of leadership and communication?

Note on Timing:

When God told Adam he would die "in the day" he ate the fruit, many struggle with the fact that Adam lived 930 years. However, 2 Peter 3:8 tells us that, "One day is with the Lord as a thousand years, and a thousand years as one day." Adam never lived a full "day" by this measure—he died within God's timeline.

Notes

_____

_____

_____

_____

_____

_____

_____

_____

_____

_____

_____

_____

—— *Chapter 4* ——

HIDDEN FAMILIES IN PARADISE?

Children in the Garden of Eden

Most churches teach that Adam and Eve had no children while in the Garden of Eden. But when we examine Scripture carefully, several passages suggest otherwise. Let's explore six pieces of textual evidence:

Evidence 1:

The Command to Multiply Genesis 1:28 records God blessing them and commanding: "Be fruitful, and multiply, and replenish the earth."

Why would God give a command that couldn't be fulfilled? The text suggests Adam and Eve understood how to be fruitful—otherwise, the command would be meaningless.

Evidence 2:

Increased Labor Pains Genesis 3:16 contains God's punishment to Eve: "I will greatly multiply thy sorrow and thy conception; in sorrow thou shalt bring forth children."

The word "multiply" suggests an increase from a previous state. If Eve had never given birth before, how could she understand what she was losing? The text implies she had previously experienced childbirth without such pain.

Evidence 3:

The Name "Mother" Genesis 3:20 explains that "Adam called his wife's name Eve; because she was the mother of all living."

Adam gave her this name when they were cast out of the garden. The title "mother" requires having given birth to children.

Evidence 4:

Cain's Fear After killing Abel, Cain worried that "every one that findeth me shall slay me" (Genesis 4:14). If Cain and Abel were the only children on earth, who was Cain afraid would kill him?

Evidence 5:

Cain's Wife Genesis 4:17 mentions that "Cain knew his wife; and she conceived, and bare Enoch: and he builded a city." Where did this wife come from if no other children existed?

Evidence 6:

The Timeline Question Genesis 5:3 states that Adam was 130 years old when Seth was born. If Adam and Eve only had three children (Cain, Abel, Seth) in 130 years, this seems inconsistent with God's command to "be fruitful and multiply."

Putting It Together:

These textual clues suggest the possibility that Adam and Eve had many children during their time in Eden. We don't know how long they lived there before the fall—the Bible doesn't specify. In a perfect environment, with perfect bodies, reproduction would have been natural and without complication.

Questions for Consideration:

- How might this perspective change our understanding of early human history?
- What does this suggest about taking every detail of Scripture seriously?
- How do we balance traditional teachings with careful textual examination?

A Note on Biblical Authority:

Some scholars dismiss these details as unimportant, saying it doesn't matter whether Adam and Eve had children in the garden. But as Jesus said in Matthew 5:18: "Till heaven and earth pass, one jot or one tittle shall in no wise pass from the law, till all be fulfilled."

Every detail of Scripture serves a purpose for our understanding and growth. When we dismiss parts of the text as irrelevant, we risk missing important insights God intended for us to discover.

Notes

_____

_____

_____

_____

_____

_____

_____

_____

_____

_____

_____

—— *Chapter 5* ——

DID JOB'S CHILDREN
REALLY DIE?

Rethinking a Familiar Tragedy

The story of Job is often told with a heartbreaking emphasis:
God allowed Satan to kill Job's children. For many, this detail
raises difficult questions about God's justice and compassion.
But what if we've been reading this passage through the lens of
translation rather than the original intent of the text?

When we look more closely at the Hebrew words used in Job
1, a different possibility emerges—one that suggests Job's children may not have been the ones who died at all.

Looking at the Text

In Job 1:8, the Lord refers to Job as His "servant." The
Hebrew word here is *eh'-bed*—a bondman or slave.

But as the narrative continues (Job 1:15–19), each messenger
who comes to Job uses a different Hebrew term when speaking
of the losses. They use the word *nah'-ar*, which refers to a child,
a lad, or a young servant.

Here's the critical point:

- Job 1:15 – "They have slain the servants (*nah'-ar*)."
- Job 1:16 – "The fire of God... burned up the sheep, and the servants (*nah'-ar*)."
- Job 1:17 – "The Chaldeans... have slain the servants (*nah'-ar*)."
- Job 1:19 – "The house fell... and it fell upon the young men (*nah'-ar*)."

In the first three reports, translators consistently chose "servants." But in verse 19, the same Hebrew word *nah'-ar* was translated as "young men." This shift in wording has led many to assume the text suddenly refers to Job's sons and daughters.

A Question of Translation

Why not remain consistent? If *nah'-ar* was translated as "servants" earlier, why change it to "young men" in verse 19? If the translation had remained uniform, we might never have concluded that Job's children were the ones who perished.

And notice something else: Job's sons and daughters were described as eating and drinking wine together in their eldest brother's house (Job 1:18). These were adults—not children. Meanwhile, the Hebrew word *nah'-ar* often describes servants or those younger in age.

Considering the Context

If Job's children had truly been killed, wouldn't his wife's reaction have been centered on that devastating loss? Yet she only seems distraught once Job himself is afflicted physically (Job 2:9). Could this silence about her children suggest they were not, in fact, dead?

This perspective doesn't diminish the trials Job endured—his suffering was still immense. But it may reshape the way we understand God's role in this story. Perhaps Job's children were spared, and the narrative has been misinterpreted because of a translator's inconsistent choice of words.

Questions for Consideration

- How does this possibility affect your understanding of Job's suffering?
- What role does careful translation play in shaping the way we interpret Scripture?
- Could this example invite us to approach other "settled" interpretations with fresh eyes?

Notes

_____

_____

_____

_____

_____

_____

_____

_____

_____

_____

_____

_____

―――― *Chapter 6* ――――

SIGNS OF JESUS CHRIST'S RETURN

Have the Seals Already Been Opened?

Few topics spark more curiosity and debate among believers than the return of Christ. Many preachers teach that the seals in Revelation remain closed and will only open after the rapture. But is that truly what Scripture reveals?

When we compare Jesus' words in Matthew 24 with the seals described in Revelation 6, we begin to see a pattern—one that suggests several seals may already have been opened.

The Disciples' Question

In Matthew 24:3, the disciples asked Jesus directly: "What shall be the sign of thy coming, and of the end of the world?" His response gave a detailed sequence of signs that believers could watch for.

Let's walk through these step by step and compare them with the first five seals of Revelation.

The First Seal: Deception

- **Matthew 24:4–5** – Jesus warns, "Take heed that no man deceive you. For many shall come in my name, saying, I am Christ; and shall deceive many."
- **Revelation 6:2** – A rider on a white horse appears, crowned and conquering, imitating Christ but not the true Messiah.

Satan has always used deception as his primary weapon. Just as he twisted God's words in the Garden of Eden, he continues to imitate Christ to mislead.

The Second Seal: Conflict and Violence

- **Matthew 24:6** – "You shall hear of wars and rumors of wars."
- **Revelation 6:4** – A red horse brings power to take peace from the earth so that people kill one another.

History is full of wars, and our present age continues this cycle—fitting the description of the second seal.

The Third Seal: Scarcity

- **Matthew 24:7** – Jesus speaks of "famines."
- **Revelation 6:5–6** – A black horse appears, carrying scales, symbolizing economic struggle and food shortages.

From ancient times to modern headlines, famine and inflation have plagued nations.

The Fourth Seal: Death

- **Matthew 24:7–8** – Jesus warns of pestilences and widespread suffering.

- **Revelation 6:7–8** – A pale horse named Death appears, bringing devastation through sword, famine, plague, and wild beasts.

Again, this aligns with what humanity has witnessed across centuries.

The Fifth Seal: Persecution

- **Matthew 24:9** – Jesus says, "Then shall they deliver you up to be afflicted, and shall kill you: and ye shall be hated of all nations for my name's sake."
- **Revelation 6:9–11** – The souls of martyrs cry out under the altar, awaiting justice for their deaths.

Believers throughout history have been persecuted and martyred for their faith, echoing this fifth seal.

The Sixth Seal: Still to Come

The sixth seal is different. Revelation 6:12–14 describes cosmic disturbances—earthquakes, the sun darkening, the moon turning to blood, and stars falling. Jesus echoes this in Matthew 24:29–30, saying these events will occur "immediately after the tribulation."

This suggests that while the first five seals may already be open, the sixth remains future—ushering in the final stage before Christ's return.

Living in Readiness

If this interpretation is true, then we are living in the midst of the sealed events. The "last days" are not merely approaching—they are already unfolding. What remains is the opening of the sixth seal, followed by the visible return of Christ in glory.

Consider This

- How does viewing the seals as already open affect your sense of urgency about faith and readiness?
- If persecution and deception are part of our present reality, how can we stay rooted in truth and hope?
- Does this reading encourage you to see prophecy not as distant speculation but as present reality?

Notes

_____

_____

_____

_____

_____

_____

_____

_____

_____

_____

_____

_____

―――― *Chapter 7* ――――

THE PLAN OF SALVATION

What Does It Mean to Be Born Again?

Opening Statement: If there is one question more important than all others, it is this: How can my name be written in the Book of Life?

This chapter is not written to condemn or criticize any religion or denomination. Rather, it is offered as an invitation to examine the Scriptures afresh and consider what Jesus Himself taught about being born again.

Jesus gave Nicodemus a clear and uncompromising answer in John 3. The path into God's kingdom is not through tradition, good works, or personal effort—but through being born again.

Jesus' Conversation with Nicodemus

- John 3:3 – Jesus says, "Except a man be born again, he cannot see the kingdom of God."
- John 3:5 – He explains further: "Except a man be born of water and of the Spirit, he cannot enter into the kingdom of God."

Nicodemus was puzzled, just as many are today. How can a person experience a second birth? Jesus pointed to two essentials: water and Spirit.

Born of Water: Baptism

Jesus commanded His disciples: "Go ye therefore, and teach all nations, baptizing them in the name of the Father, and of the Son, and of the Holy Ghost" (Matthew 28:19).

But notice carefully—He spoke of a name, not names. Throughout Scripture, that name is revealed as Jesus:

• The Son came in the Father's name (John 5:43).
• The Holy Spirit was sent in Jesus' name (John 14:26).
• The apostles were baptized in the name of Jesus Christ (Acts 2:38; Acts 10:48).

Thus, baptism in Jesus' name is not a mere ritual—it is an entry into covenant with Him. Without repentance and this baptism, water alone is just getting wet.

Born of the Spirit: The Gift of the Holy Ghost

Jesus compared the Spirit's work to the wind: invisible, mysterious, yet heard (John 3:8). On the day of Pentecost, this took the form of a sound—a rushing mighty wind—and believers spoke in new tongues (Acts 2:2–4).

The evidence of the Spirit is not merely a feeling; it is a sound. Everyone born of the Spirit demonstrates it by speaking in tongues as the Spirit gives utterance. This isn't reserved for a select few or an ancient generation—Jesus said, "so is everyone that is born of the Spirit."

A Gift of Faith, Not Works

Receiving the Spirit is not about striving, fasting, or achieving. It is a gift received by faith. If you already believe in the unseen God, you already have the faith to receive His Spirit. Speaking in tongues is not faking—it is faith in action.

This walk is about faith, not feelings. Some mornings you may not feel God's presence, but that does not mean He is absent. As Paul reminds us: "We walk by faith, not by sight" (2 Corinthians 5:7).

Why It Matters

The apostles did not present multiple ways to salvation. Peter proclaimed with boldness:

"Neither is there salvation in any other: for there is none other name under heaven given among men, whereby we must be saved" (Acts 4:12).

There is one Lord, one faith, and one baptism (Ephesians 4:5). The way is narrow, but it is also simple: repentance, baptism in Jesus' name, and receiving the Spirit.

Reflection Questions

- Why is baptism in the name of Jesus emphasized so strongly in Scripture?
- What does it mean to walk by faith, not by feelings, in daily Christian life?
- How does understanding the Spirit as a gift change the way we approach prayer and worship?

Notes

_____

_____

_____

_____

_____

_____

_____

_____

_____

_____

_____

_____

Chapter 8

MY PERSONAL TESTIMONY

How God Transforms a Broken Life

Scripture is full of examples where God transforms broken lives into vessels of hope. My story is one of those transformations. I share it not to draw attention to myself, but to point you toward the God who never gave up on me.

A Difficult Beginning

I grew up in a home where love was absent. I was one of seven children—one brother and five sisters—and instead of unity, we lived in conflict and pain. Abuse was common. My father disciplined us harshly, sometimes beating us until we bled, often in front of neighbors. My mother, though religious, dismissed my desire to follow God. When I told her I wanted to be baptized at seventeen, she called me an idiot and refused to attend.

At that time, my self-worth was almost nonexistent. By my senior year of high school, my GPA was just 1.67. I wondered if my life had any meaning at all.

Meeting God's Love

But then God broke through. At seventeen, I gave my life to Him. I discovered a love that no family or friend had ever shown me. Even when loneliness overwhelmed me and I considered ending my life, God met me in that dark place. He spoke to me, saying He would be my friend. From that moment, my life changed forever.

In time, God blessed me with a loving wife—the best and most beautiful gift I could have asked for. I married at age thirty-one, and the wait was worth it. He also gave me the honor of serving in the Army for ten years, where I learned perseverance and discipline.

Walking With God

Over the years, God has worked through me in ways that still amaze me. I have prayed for the sick and seen them healed. I once prayed for a dead man, and he came back to life. God has also given me visions, dreams, and even out-of-body experiences—all reminders that His Spirit is alive and active.

I admit that even now, some wounds from my childhood linger. But God continues to heal me, layer by layer. His grace not only rescued me—it sustains me daily.

Growing in Understanding

There were times when I struggled to understand Scripture. For example, in Luke 7:19–22, Jesus' message to John's disciples puzzled me. He spoke of the blind seeing, the lame walking, lepers being cleansed, and the dead raised. At first, I thought: Satan can heal, too—what makes this different?

It took years of prayer before God revealed the deeper meaning. Jesus wasn't merely describing physical miracles; He was pointing to spiritual transformation. Those blind to truth were given sight. Those crippled by sin could walk in freedom. Those covered in guilt were cleansed. The spiritually dead were raised to life—something Satan could never do.

This revelation reminded me of Isaiah 55:8–9: "For my thoughts are not your thoughts, neither are your ways my ways, saith the Lord. For as the heavens are higher than the earth, so are my ways higher than your ways, and my thoughts than your thoughts."

Understanding comes only as God chooses to reveal it. That's why the relationship matters more than religious knowledge. If we approach Him humbly, He will open our eyes.

Personal Application

- How has God's love transformed the broken areas of your life?
- In what ways do you need to hear His voice reminding you, *"I will be your friend"*?
- What personal struggles might become testimonies of His grace?

Notes

_____

_____

_____

_____

_____

_____

_____

_____

_____

_____

_____

—— *Chapter 9* ——

BONUS – A THEORY ON DINOSAURS

Could Creation Hold an Overlooked Mystery?

Many people wonder where dinosaurs fit into the story of creation. We can't deny their existence—fossils and museum displays bear clear witness. Yet scientists often claim these creatures lived millions of years ago, while the Bible presents humanity's history as spanning roughly six to seven thousand years. How can we reconcile these views?

Let's take a closer look at Scripture and consider a possibility.

A Question in Genesis

Genesis 1:1 says, "In the beginning God created the heavens and the earth." Yet in the very next verse we read: "And the earth was without form, and void; and darkness was upon the face of the deep."

Doesn't that raise a question? If God created the heavens and the earth in verse 1, why does verse 2 describe the earth as empty and void? It's like someone telling you, "I built a house," and then showing you an empty lot. Something appears to have happened in between.

The Firmament Shift

Notice also that in the beginning the earth was in God's immediate presence. But on the second day of creation, God established a firmament—separating the earth from His presence (Genesis 1:6–8). Could this separation hint at a dramatic shift between verse 1 and verse 2?

Ezekiel's Clue

Ezekiel 28:11–19 describes an anointed cherub—Satan—who once walked in the Garden of Eden before his fall. This raises another question: how could he have been there before Adam and Eve? Scripture doesn't suggest two Gardens of Eden, so what does this mean?

Here's a possible answer: the first creation in Genesis 1:1 may have belonged to Lucifer. Isaiah 14:13 records his boast: "I will exalt my throne above the stars of God." Thrones represent kingdoms, and it's possible God created a kingdom for him—including the dinosaurs—just as He later created animals for Adam.

But when iniquity was found in Lucifer, God cast him out and destroyed that first creation with water. Then, much later, He destroyed the earth again with Noah's flood.

A Spiritual Connection

If this is true, it might explain why Satan continues to resist humanity so fiercely. He lost his kingdom and his throne, and God gave dominion to mankind instead. Perhaps this fuels his ongoing attempts to deceive and destroy.

Just Food for Thought

You don't have to believe this interpretation—it's a personal theory meant to stir reflection. What matters most is not speculation, but that each of us seeks God for ourselves.

My prayer is that you let these ideas provoke you to study, ask questions, and deepen your relationship with the Lord. Be original—just as God created you to be.

Notes

_____

_____

_____

_____

_____

_____

_____

_____

_____

_____

_____